ROLE-PLAYING FOR FUN AND PROFIT™

COSPLAY

JENNIFER CULP

W9-BUI-561

rosen publishing's
rosen
central®
New York

Published in 2016 by The Rosen Publishing Group, Inc.
29 East 21st Street, New York, NY 10010

Copyright © 2016 by The Rosen Publishing Group, Inc.

First Edition

Library of Congress Cataloging-in-Publication Data

Culp, Jennifer, 1985–
 Cosplay / Jennifer Culp. — First edition.
    pages cm. — (Role-playing for fun and profit)
 Includes bibliographical references and index.
 ISBN 978-1-4994-3714-0 (library bound) — ISBN 978-1-4777-8761-8 (pbk.) — ISBN 978-1-4994-3713-3 (6-pack)
 1. Cosplay—Juvenile literature. I. Title.
 GV1201.8.C85 2016
 793.93—dc23
                              2015024809

Manufactured in the United States of America

CONTENTS

INTRODUCTION

Batman. Wonder Woman. Master Chief, Mario, and Lara Croft. Many people have wondered, "What would it be like to be my hero, just for one day?" Cosplay, the art of crafting and wearing an elaborate costume based on a favorite character or an original design, allows them to find out. Cosplay, short for "costume play," is internationally popular, and people of all ages, sexes, ethnicities, and body types enjoy dressing up to attend fan conventions and events.

Most people cosplay for fun, rather than profit, but some particularly dedicated individuals have found ways to turn their passion for the craft into a way to earn money. Mel Hoppe, who works under the moniker WindoftheStars Cosplay, began cosplaying in 2004. With over ninety costumes created for her personal résumé in the last decade, she takes commissions for custom work from fellow fans, does freelance costume work for established companies, and is paid for convention appearances and sponsored promotional work. Catherine Lewis, owner of God Save the Queen Fashions, LLC, formerly worked as a seamstress, performing simple alterations before progressing to Halloween costumes and repairs for drag queens' performance wear. She took her first cosplay commission in January 2008. "I was so excited to have found something that combines so many of my passions!" she wrote on her website. "Now, with a small team of talented artisans, GSTQ Fashions produces numerous high-quality costumes for both fans and

Cosplayers who resemble the character they imitate provide a particularly convincing illusion!

costume connoisseurs alike all year round." Yaya Han, a costume designer and creator who works as a cosplay entertainer and guest at conventions and events, also markets a line of cosplay accessories and created her own collection of Yaya Han Brand merchandising.

Cosplay as a career, however, is still a budding development. The opportunity to make an adequate living as a professional cosplay model is still quite rare, limited to a few well-known cosplayers who have already gained fan followings prior to earning money from corporate sponsorships and appearances. Other cosplay professionals earn money by working as professional costumers, using their skills to create commissioned costumes for other individuals or companies.

CHAPTER ONE

A HISTORY OF COSPLAY

In July 1939, one year after Superman made his national debut in *Action Comics #1* and thirty-eight years before *Star Wars* aired in theaters, the First World Science Fiction Convention (known as Worldcon) was held in Manhattan, New York. Two of the two hundred fans in attendance made history when they arrived quite literally wearing their passion for sci-fi on their bodies. Forrest J. Ackerman and his companion, Myrtle R. "Morojo" Jones,

Forrest J. Ackerman, one of history's first cosplayers, fortunately did not die at the hands of his extensive prop collection.

MOROJO, THE MOTHER OF COSPLAY

Myrtle Rebecca Jones first met Forrest J. Ackerman at a meeting for Esperanto speakers. In Esperanto, an international language created in the late 1800s, her initials were "Morojo," and she went by the nickname in sci-fi and fantasy circles. According to Eric Leif Davin, author of *Partners in Wonder,* the costumes Morojo created for herself and Ackerman made a big splash: "'Morojo,' dressed in supposed twenty-fifth century fashion, made a big impression on New York fans at the First World Science Fiction Convention in 1939." In 1940, she was asked to write about women and science fiction for *Science Fiction* magazine and expressed her confidence that other women would soon be writing in to discuss the genre as well. Along with Ackerman, she edited the fanzine *Voice of the Imagi-Nation* for almost ten years, and edited and published her own Esperanto-focused zine from 1941 to 1958. She attended other conventions in costume, wearing a frog facemask created by future famed monster animator Ray Harryhausen in 1941, and "created a sensation as A. Merritt's Snake Mother" at Pacificon 1946, Ackerman remembered.

Though Morojo and Ackerman had broken up and married other people years before, Ackerman and other friends published a remembrance zine in her honor when she passed away from cancer in 1964. "I remember Morojo," he wrote, "as the greatest female fanne [sic] who ever lived."

came dressed in original "futuristicostumes" designed and created by Morojo. Their caped costumes were based on outfits worn by actors in the 1936 movie *Things to Come*. Ackerman and Morojo looked like space-faring superheroes and started a new trend of dressing up among sci-fi fans. By the next year, fan costuming had gained enough popularity that the second Worldcon featured a small costume masquerade, which became a yearly tradition. "It was pretty informal," remembered Mike Resnick, author of *Always a Fan*. "But then the costuming bug struck, and costumes began getting more elaborate."

In the following decades, many people attended Worldcon masquerades in elaborate costumes. Some attended in nonexistent costumes! Sci-fi fan and author Ron Miller recalled that at conventions in the 1970s there were, "an awful lot of naked people (which eventually resulted in the only rule I ever remember seeing posted: 'No costume is no costume.')" Worldcon adopted another rule banning food items from costuming after a memorable occurrence at Worldcon 1972 when a man arrived dressed in gallons of peanut butter that turned rancid after a few hours. The peanut butter disaster didn't destroy fans' enthusiasm for dressing up, however, and in 1974 San Diego Comic-Con (now one of the largest comic entertainment conventions in North America) added a masquerade costume contest to its schedule of events.

Around the mid-seventies, fan costuming also began to gain popularity in Japan, propelled by the success of anime series such as *Mobile Suit Gundam* throughout the eighties. A TV series about a soccer team, *Captain Tsubasa*, spread the appeal of fan costuming in Japan even further thanks to the relative ease of creating a soccer uniform. Other simple costumes, such as school uniforms, also provided a gateway into

Millions of people around the world empathize with fictional characters. Cosplay allows humans to enact these fantasies.

the hobby for those who wanted to dress up but didn't have the skills to build a giant robot costume.

In 1984, the worlds of American and Japanese fans collided when Japanese writer Takahashi Nobuyuki attended the 42nd annual Worldcon in Los Angeles, California. Nobuyuki was so impressed by the costumed fans he saw at the convention that he wrote about them for his Japanese readers. To describe the phenomenon of fans dressing up in costume, Nobuyuki coined a new phrase: "costume play," which was eventually shortened to "cosplay." Now the hobby of dressing up in a costume had a name, and people who enjoyed attending conventions in costumes became known as "cosplayers."

GEEK GOES MAINSTREAM

As home computers and access to the Internet became more readily available in the 1990s, a sort of cross-cultural pollination began to take place. Western superheroes became better known in Japan, and American geeks discovered Japanese anime series such as *Sailor Moon*. Fans on opposite sides of the world met through online message boards, which made it easy to share thoughts and images. Websites and message boards replaced fan zines—small, self-published magazines made and shared between fans, which old-school fans like Forrest J. Ackerman used to communicate with each other—and made it much easier for science fiction and fantasy enthusiasts to talk about their interests.

Throughout the 1990s, geek culture continued to blossom. Bill Gates and Steve Jobs changed the face of computing forever.

Cosplay allows anyone to step into the shoes of characters of legend, whether they choose the Empire or the Republic from *Star Wars*.

Star Wars returned with *The Phantom Menace*, and comic properties such as *X-Men* and *Spider-Man* reached new audiences with the release of successful movies. Manga and anime became increasingly popular in the Western world, spurred by series such as *Sailor Moon*. By 2010, twenty-year-olds who were born in the nineties couldn't remember a world where being labeled a "nerd" was a social stigma. This cultural shift affected the perception of cosplay as well. In previous decades, the thought of a grown adult dressing up in a superhero costume for fun was considered odd. By 2000, it didn't seem quite so strange to the general public. In 2003, the first World Cosplay Summit was held in Nagoya, Japan.

BANISHING "BOOTH BABES"

The 1990s also saw a backlash against the custom of companies employing so-called "booth babes"—scantily clad promotional models—to promote their products at events such as the Electronic Entertainment Expo (E3). E3 is a professional industry event, rather than a fan convention, but the tone it set and hiring practices it perpetuated had—and still have—a major influence over video game fan culture. In 2006, E3 announced that it would begin enforcing long-neglected rules of conduct and attire for spokesmodels on its convention floor, banning partial nudity and "bathing-suit bottoms that were once seen as almost standard booth-babe attire," according to Jonathan Silverstein of ABCNews. This was hailed as good news by industry professionals and fans who criticized the hiring and display of bikini-clad female models as sexist. However, it was only a first step toward addressing the underlying problem of sexism in nerd culture. As the very concept of "booth babes" itself demonstrates, tech and geek entertainment marketing was aimed almost exclusively at men. Video game marketing has changed over the years, transforming from family-focused ads that showed girls and women enjoying games alongside men to misogynist, male-catering commercials that presented women as whiny nags or compliant babes. Though women such as

Morojo had been active in nerdy activities and social groups from the beginning, in the nineties an ugly, marketing-driven notion began to take hold: Women couldn't be real fans, "real" gamers, or "real" geeks. Women, the presence of booth babes at conventions had suggested, were just there for decoration. This dangerous attitude affected the perception of female cosplayers, with many men assuming they weren't "real" fans of the characters they dressed as and accusing them of dressing in costume "just to get attention."

By 2010, women cosplayers were sick and tired of inappropriate comments, unwanted touching, and rude convention-goers taking sexually objectifying photos without asking for permission. "Cosplay is not consent" became a popular catchphrase by 2013, with a popular Tumblr of the same name gathering reports of instances of harassment and abuse to call attention to the problem and bring it to convention organizers' attention. "Cosplay is not consent" now appears in bold in New York Comic Con's anti-harassment policy. "Keep your hands to yourself. If you would like to take a picture with or of another NYCC Fan, always ask first and respect that person's right to say no. When at NYCC, be respectful, be nice, be cool and be kind to each other," the policy goes on to say. "The number of 'con creepers' may be growing, but cosplayers may now feel more open dishing about 'con creepers.'" Pacific Media Expo's Amanda Badillo told *LA Weekly* in 2013: "Knowing that they aren't alone, [women cosplayers] are more likely to open up to friends and groups on the Internet as to the kinds of 'creepers' they've dealt with, warn others about 'serial creepers' and giving advice as to how to deal with them."

When a cosplayer wears a skimpy costume, it doesn't mean he or she is looking for a proposition. Remember, people in costumes are people.

Cosplay is currently pushing the boundaries for acceptance in other areas. As The Verge writer Adrianne Jeffries noted, "Some fans will badger cosplayers who don't have the same body type as their characters, or try to play a character of a different race." In an effort to stem the tide of mean-spirited anonymous online comments and prejudice, some cosplay hobbyists have begun grassroots movements to encourage body positivity and diversity in cosplay. The Tumblr page "Cosplaying While Black" showcases the work of dark-skinned cosplayers of all skill levels. Other fan-run Tumblr accounts such as "Chubby Cosplay" offer platforms to encourage self-acceptance and celebrate cool costumes created and worn by people who aren't thin. The hashtags #cospositive and #bodypositivecosplay highlight the work of cosplayers with diverse body types on social media.

CHAPTER TWO

COSPLAY TODAY

In 2006, 15,000 people attended the first New York City Comic Con. Eight years later, more than 151,000 guests attended NYCC 2014, making it the largest comic book and pop culture convention in the United States. In the days following the convention, publications such as *Business Insider*, the *Daily Beast*, and *People* published "Best Of" photo galleries of the attending cosplayers on their websites. And that's just one of dozens of cons held annually in the United States, along with San Diego Comic-Con International, Wizard World Chicago, WonderCon, Anime Expo, Fanime, Comikaze, and Dragon*Con, among numerous other regional conventions both large and small!

CONS AND COSTUMES

Cons are where cosplayers go to debut new costumes, network with fellow fans, and be photographed in costume. Some cons host cosplay contests, which provide recognition and monetary rewards to cosplayers who excel at their craft. Cons provide

Cosplay is a sure-fire way to meet other enthusiasts! Someone dressed up in a costume from your favorite game or show will likely be happy to talk about it!

commission opportunities for professional cosplay costumers and a place for well-known cosplayers and costume creators to sell prints and merchandise as vendors. At some cons, companies sponsor professional cosplay models to encourage fan interaction and promote their products. Since the first-ever futuristicostume was worn at Worldcon, conventions and cosplay have enjoyed a symbiotic relationship: cosplay is an essential component of con culture, and cons give cosplay a venue in which to flourish.

Many well-known cosplayers cite the experience of attending a convention as the source of their interest in the hobby.

Cosplayer Linda Le puts hundreds of hours of work into each individual costume.

Pro cosplay model Lindsay Elyse started cosplaying at age thirteen after her mother convinced her to attend the AniZona convention in her home state of Arizona. "I have no social skills and I was horrified," Elyse said in an interview with Kaila White of *The Arizona Republic,* "then this group of girls walks by and they have bright blue hair and big swords and my mom looks at me like, 'Are you ready now?'" Yaya Han learned about cosplay while preparing to attend her first Anime Expo in 1999. Finding photos of anime-costumed attendees online, Han was immediately attracted to cosplay: "What better way to show my childhood love for the anime/manga fandom than to 'become' my favorite characters?" she wrote. Cosplay comedian D Piddy, who is known for appearing as his irreverent dancing interpretation of the "Merc With a Mouth" character Deadpool at ten to fifteen conventions per year, lists Fanime in San José, California, New York Comic Con, and Comic-Con International in San Diego, California as his personal favorite cons. "They all have their different reasons why, but out of all the cons I've been to,

PROS WHO PLAY

Not everyone who cosplays is a professional cosplayer, but professionals who work in other roles in "geeky" industries sometimes cosplay! Mark Meer, a video game voice actor, appears at conventions in costume as Commander Shepard of *Mass Effect*, one of his best-known voice roles. Rana McAnear, whose face was used as the model for another of *Mass Effect's* characters, Samara, also makes appearances as her character in a stunningly lifelike costume. *Heroes of Cosplay's* Jessica Merizan worked as a community manager for BioWare, and Meagan Marie of Crystal Dynamics is another well-known cosplay hobbyist.

those are my favorite," he said in an interview with Barbara Steigerwald for the When Nerds Attack website.

THE CONS OF CON

Star cosplayers are not typically paid substantially to attend conventions, however. When invited as the guest of a con—with his or her face and name appearing on promotional materials and perhaps offered a panel on which to discuss and promote his or her work—a cosplayer is more often provided with a payment to cover some of the travel and hotel expenses and given a booth on the convention floor to sell prints and/or products. However, this is no guarantee that the special guest cosplayer will sell any merchandise at all. In this case, the cosplayer would be lucky to break even on the travel and food costs necessitated by attending the con and would receive no compensation for the time, expense, and expertise that went into making a costume *or* the time spent working a booth at the con, not to mention the upfront costs of preparing prints and merchandise for sale. Some pro cosplayers negotiate sales guarantees with the conventions they attend to protect themselves from this situation. In these cases, the con agrees that the cosplayer must sell a certain amount of merchandise to compensate them for their attendance. If the cosplayer's booth sales don't meet this goal, the con covers the difference. Even with a sales guarantee, however, a star cosplay guest isn't necessarily raking in a truckload of cash from a convention appearance. At this point in the evolution of cosplay, most well-known North American cosplayers indicate that the money they earn feeds directly back into their continuing cosplay expenses. Very few cosplayers currently earn enough money from sponsored appearances to support themselves full-time.

Con culture can pose another problem for well-known (and casual) cosplayers: harassment. A "Psychology of Cosplay" survey created by clinical psychologists Dr. Andrea Letamendi and Dr. Robin Rosenberg collected data from nearly one thousand cosplayers over a period of months in 2013. Of that population, almost 75 percent were female. Lisa Granshaw, writer for the Daily Dot, pointed out, "This would make [cosplay] one of the few areas in geek culture where women dominate." Rob Salkowitz, author of *Comic-Con and the Business of Pop Culture*, agreed in an NBC Bay Area website interview with Colin Bertram. "The women who come to comic and fan conventions are twice as likely to be dressing up as the guys," he explained to Bertram. Their greater numbers do not necessarily make women in costume feel safe or welcome at a con, however, when "con creepers" roam through conventions taking illegal photos, making lewd insults and propositions, or trying to grab or touch cosplayers. Harassment and alienation isn't just a problem for women wearing revealing costumes, either. The participants in Dr. Letamandi and Rosenberg's survey overwhelmingly identified as white, with very small percentages of Latino or Hispanic, Asian, African American or black, and mixed ethnicity cosplayers included in the survey. According to Granshaw, cosplayer Chaka Cumberbatch, a member of Letamandi and Rosenberg's "Psychology of Cosplay" panel at GeekGirlCon 2013, spoke about feeling like "the odd kid out" because of her dark skin color, because the popular perception of a "nerd" is typically a white man. "There is a lot of bullying that goes on," cosplayer and Comic-Con attendee Lawrence Brenner said in an interview with Colin Bertram, noting that cosplayers have been bullied on the basis of body type, ethnicity, and sexuality.

But cosplayers aren't resigned to accept this sort of inappropriate treatment. The "cosplay is not consent" movement continues to raise awareness and educate con-goers on how to interact appropriately and respectfully with cosplayers at cons. "I think things are getting better [for minorities], but there's always room for improvement," Cumberbatch told Granshaw, before going on to point out that increased diversity in geeky properties helps to promote increased acceptance and diversity among fandoms. Many convention organizers are listening to cosplayers' concerns and making a point to publish and enforce anti-harassment policies. "Big consumer brands can't afford

Chaka Cumberbatch (*right*) poses dressed as Wonder Woman at the 2013 Comic-Con International convention.

to be associated with events where a convention space is known to be uncomfortable," Salkowitz told Bertram. As the popularity of cosplay grows, conventions have a real motivation to prohibit harassment and ensure cosplayers' safety, comfort, and continued attendance.

In spite of some old-school comic artists' grumbling (both Tony Harris, who worked on *Starman* and *Ex Machina*, and Pat Broderick of *Micronauts* and *Batman: Year Three* published cruel and dismissive comments about cosplayers in 2014), cosplayers remain undeterred by negativity. As Sam Maggs sarcastically responded in an article for the website the Mary Sue, "Cool, stop going to the biggest conventions in the world, then. I bet that'll really help your bottom line. Good luck with that." The hobby is becoming increasingly popular among a diverse group of people. Cosplay is here to stay.

CHAPTER THREE

PLAYING DRESS UP FOR A LIVING: CAREERS IN COSPLAY

An online search of "how to become a professional cosplayer" brings up a common response on many websites and forums: "there is no such thing as a professional cosplayer." This isn't true, necessarily, but the familiar refrain is most likely intended to convey realistic expectations: in North America, few individuals earn the bulk of their living solely from making and wearing costumes. Many well-known cosplayers work another job to support themselves while the money they earn from cosplay appearances and print sales goes back into funding new costume materials and labor, travel costs, photography, and other cosplay-related expenses. There are certainly opportunities to make money in cosplay, but they require a great deal of hard work and luck. "You really have to love cosplay. There's no money to be made here. You're pretty much making enough money to make a costume," cosplay star Linda Le frankly stated

THE MODEL COSPLAYER

While cosplay as a hobby is increasingly friendly to different genders, ages, and body types, physicality is a major limiting factor for aspiring cosplayers looking to do appearances and promotional work for video game or comic companies. This sort of cosplay work is much more akin to professional modeling than any other profession. Most cosplayers who are hired to promote games or products are young, thin, and female. Additionally, a strong resemblance to a specific character may be required. In late 2012, Irrational Games hired

Russian cosplayer Anna Moleva to portray a character from their upcoming game *BioShock Infinite* to promote the game based on Moleva's uncanny resemblance to the character. (Many cosplay models already have large fan followings based on their previous cosplay work.) Compared to other professions, the barrier for entry into cosplay modeling is high, and very few people do it full-time. "Think about it this way: how many people move to Hollywood every year to become a famous actor? How many actually do? Not many. Most of these people have to have a regular job to pay rent as acting (just like cosplay) is not a steady paycheck," wrote well-known cosplay hobbyist Abby Dark-Star.

Pros and Cons of Pro Cosplay

Professional cosplayer Lindsay Elyse, who started cosplaying as a hobby at age thirteen, is one of the lucky few who works full-time as a professional cosplayer, making appearances at conventions, selling photo prints, and live streaming games as a member of Astro Gaming's Astro Stream Team. In addition to Astro, her game streaming is sponsored by Cellucor and Gunnar Optiks. In 2013 and 2014, Elyse was hired to portray specific characters at conventions by multiple companies, working with Ubisoft to promote *Watch_Dogs* at San Diego Comic-Con 2013, with 2K to promote *Borderlands: The Presequel* at SDCC 2014 and CAPCOM to portray the character Poison at the

Although cosplayer Linda Le gains loads of exposure for her cosplay efforts, she gets little in the way of a paycheck.

same event, with TriForce to portray Wonder Woman and Master Chief at New York Comic Con 2014, and by Bethesda to portray the character Tatiana at GameStop Expo 2014, among others. Elyse makes her own costumes for these appearances.

In an "Ask Me Anything" thread on Reddit in 2014, Elyse was questioned about how, exactly, professional cosplayers get paid for their work. "It's kind of all over the place!" she answered. "We get appearance fees sometimes, we get products sometimes, we get things like travel and food stipends in exchange for work. I've even had companies agree to pay me by bringing a friend of mine to a convention with me. I make extra money by selling prints online and at convention booths as well! You sort of get hired randomly and never really have a set income. It's kind of exciting, but also scary!" Elyse noted that this may be different for other pro cosplayers and also stated that the range of payment varies widely from event to event. There are few set industry standards in place to regulate wages and hiring practices for pro cosplayers, as there are for fashion models, though agency representation is becoming more common for big-name cosplayers.

There is debate over who, exactly, could be considered the first professional cosplayer, but one name looms large: Jessica Nigri. Nigri began cosplaying in 2009, when she attended San Diego Comic-Con dressed as "Sexy Pikachu," a bikini-clad version of a popular Pokémon character. A photo of her costume went viral and vaulted Nigri, quite unexpectedly, into cosplay superstardom. She began selling pin-up style photo prints of herself in costume online in 2010, a practice Nigri pioneered, and began making paid appearances in costume on behalf of

Pro cosplay model Jessica Nigri started out building costumes for fun, but now spends hundreds of hours creating realistic costumes to represent video game brands.

game companies in 2012. Nigri is also credited with changing the game, so to speak, in terms of timing. Previously, cosplayers would most often create costumes for games, comics, or shows they were already familiar with and loved. Nigri, however, starts working on a costume as soon as images of characters from an upcoming game become available. This allows her to release images of costumes in conjunction with the game's release, attracting the attention of video game companies. (Now this practice is so common that many upcoming games release detailed images for the benefit of cosplayers as soon as a game is announced.) By 2013, Nigri was able to quit her grocery store job and support herself by cosplaying full-time. That doesn't mean the job is easy, however. Nigri works twelve-hour days to craft the costumes she wears for paid appearances. Each costume takes about fifty hours of work to create and costs around $500 in materials. She travels to about twenty comic conventions a year and ships photos to customers herself.

There are other downsides to making a living as a cosplay model, most notably harassment. In her Reddit "Ask Me Anything" session, Lindsay Elyse admitted that cruelty from strangers online can be crushing, sometimes causing her to avoid live-streaming games. The more well-known a cosplayer is, the more negative attention she or he is likely to attract, and it is extremely difficult to ignore a constant barrage of mean-spirited comments and threats. Jessica Nigri's father talked about the importance of keeping the family's home address private—Jessica is often recognized out in the street, and the family has had to deal with keeping real-world stalkers at bay.

The world of professional cosplay and costuming isn't all bleak, however, nor is it impossible to break into the field. Costumer Jez Roth, who formerly went by "Jezeroth," started cosplaying in the late 1990s and fell in love with the craft of costume making. Today, he continues to cosplay as a hobbyist and makes costumes professionally. He has designed and created costumes for Cirque du Soleil, the Electric Daisy Carnival, films, nightclubs, music videos, and numerous anime cons. JoEllen Elam, who became interested in costume design and

CRABCAT INDUSTRIES

"Crabcat Industries was born in a garage and started as a make-believe way to feel like we could take our dreams by the horns—of course, we later got caught up in the fantasy and actually made it reality," explains Jessica Merizan. Merizan, a trained archaeologist and anthropologist who works in the video game industry, and her best friend, Holly Conrad—artist, professional monster-maker, and cosplayer—appeared together in a documentary about their cosplay activities in 2010. The experience inspired them to "take our cosplay to another realm," as Conrad put it, and pool their talents to form Crabcat Industries and promote the art of cosplay. Merizan and Conrad create costumes, make appearances at conventions, and teach costume creation techniques on their website and You-Tube channel. In 2013, the pair appeared on the SyFy show *Heroes of Cosplay*, sharing their knowledge and passion with a broader audience.

Many convention attendees, such as Ryan Tessier and Kelly Alice Cotton, dress up for love of character and craft.

creation in 2002, has crafted "literally hundreds" of costumes and props for individuals and film and television productions. Elam's work turns her clients into fairies, mermaids, and fantastical creatures. She even creates a special bridal line for women who truly want to look like fairy princesses on their big day.

FOLLOW YOUR BLISS

The common thread between all cosplay professionals is a passion for and dedication to the craft of costume creation. "When I started cosplaying [in 1999], the U.S. community was so small and underground that we had no option of buying costumes, accessories or props. If you wanted to cosplay, you pretty much had to make the costume. I'm glad that I discovered cosplay during such a time, because it forced me to get hands on with creating costumes from scratch, and I fell in love with the craftsmanship process as much as I did with the characters," Yaya Han writes on her website. Cosplayer Jessica Merizan (also known as "Jessica Marzipan"), says, "Like any other art form, cosplay takes dedication and passion and being able to see the light at the end of the tunnel when it's discouraging or there's a challenge to overcome. But, if you are doing it and it's not fun, you need to re-evaluate the situation. Don't take yourself too seriously." She also says, "No matter what, we're all trying to chase that feeling of being someone else. Capture that feeling and don't worry about anyone else. You be that super hero or villain or obscure character! Follow your bliss!"

CHAPTER FOUR

THE CRAFT OF COSPLAY

A "costume," according to the Merriam-Webster dictionary, is "an outfit worn to create the appearance characteristic of a particular period, person, place, or thing." No matter how complicated a particular costume may be, or what material it is made from, ultimately a costume is a collection of garments: pieces of clothing meant to be worn on the body.

STITCH IT, GLUE IT, PRINT IT, BUILD IT

When it comes to creating professional-grade cosplay costumes, sewing is an essential skill. Well-known cosplayer Linda Le, who goes by the stage name "Vampy," had a leg up when she started making costumes: she learned how to sew when she was just four. Internationally famous cosplay star Yaya Han, who was featured on the SyFy show *Heroes of Cosplay*, writes on her website that she started out with "a used $40 sewing machine and a sewing book from a thrift store." Professional designer, costumer, and cosplayer Jez Roth, who has created costumes for Cirque du Soleil, offered this advice for

Sewing an entire costume might seem intimidating at first, but online tutorials can help break the most complex costume down into components.

beginning cosplayers: "Purchase a bolt of muslin when it's on sale at either Jo-Ann's or Hancock [fabric stores], buy a sewing 101 book or take a basic course, and practice general stitching and hems."

SIMPLE START

Mastering the craft of sewing may be difficult, but getting started is simple: a quick Google search of "sewing tutorial cosplay" brings up thousands of results, both general and tailored to specific designs, including detailed blog posts and instructional videos that explain how to use basic sewing equipment and piece together a garment. With a small amount of research, it's not difficult to locate local group or one-on-one sewing instruction. Costume-based businesses such as God Save the Queen Fashions in Atlanta, Georgia, and RESOBOX Gallery in Long Island City, New York, offer classes in general sewing basics and specific skills such as draping fabric on a dress form and sewing with advanced materials such as spandex and leather. Seeking out local classes is a helpful option for beginners, allowing for immediate, knowledgeable feedback from instructors and access to equipment that may be too expensive to purchase when they're just starting out.

Skill in pattern design is another cosplay must. Commercial patterns for day-to-day clothing are easily purchased. While these can be altered to meet the criteria of simple costume creation, many costumes are just too complicated or out-of-the-ordinary to rely on alteration of pre-existing patterns for their creation. As with sewing, pattern-making resources abound online. There are thousands of free tutorials, books, and local classes to help interested beginners learn. Additionally, websites such as Cosplay.com gather resources to make cosplay-specific tutorials easy to find to learn to create patterns for petticoats, boot covers, cloaks, simple armors, and wearable wings.

CONNECTING OVER THE MORE COMPLEX

Most cosplayers learn and expand their skill sets by creating progressively more difficult costumes with each successive project and, most important of all, by communicating and collaborating with each other. "Overall we cosplay to connect," wrote Linda Le, discussing a collaborative project she undertook with cosplayer and video game industry professional Meagan Marie in 2012. To bring characters from the manga series *Claymore* to life, the two women sought out the help of experts and learned to cut, assemble, and vacuform carbon fiber into shoulder pauldrons, cut and form wire mesh into structural support for cast armor pieces, and cast urethane to make the resulting costumes look as realistic as possible. "Spending a weekend geeking out with like-minded individu-

This cosplayer went to extraordinary effort to bring the armor of the Dark Lord Sauron from the classic story *Lord of the Rings* to life.

als, troubleshooting construction techniques, and playing with power tools is my idea of R&R," Marie stated.

Ultimately, the look of each specific costume drives the selection of materials and processes necessary to realize the cosplay as a finished vision. Worbla, a thermoplastic that can be molded and shaped like clay with the application of heat, is a popular material for creating realistic-looking but wearable armor. Craft foam and Wonderflex are other commonly used thermoplastics. Though they cannot be molded into smooth curves as easily as Worbla, other materials offer advantages in expense and durability. Spandex is a necessity for many superhero costumes, and leather or faux leather is required to attain rugged *Lord of the Rings*–style realness. Felt or faux fur might be used as a lining, and plastic or resin may be cast into the shape of armor scales, jewelry, or accessories. Pro Jez Roth's favorite material? Vinyl. "You can get some incredible dimensions and angles out of it that you really can't get out of other fabrics. You can distress, melt it, manipulate it into such crazy shapes as well. Stitching, paint, and surface decorations really pop on it. And it forces you to really take your time stitching as well since it's such an unforgiving fabric," he said.

3D PRINTING

Other cosplayers are pushing the boundaries of costume creation by using 3D printing technology. Stevie Dee, a United Kingdom–based cosplayer and founder of the business Crimson Coscrafts, collaborated with Tundra Designs and Gauntlet FX—companies that create high-end special effects props—to create a stunningly realistic version of the Dark Knight Batsuit earned by gamers who beat the game *Batman: Arkham Origins* with 100 percent completion. Dee meticulously designed the suit himself and did all 3D modeling work for the project. Gauntlet FX provided molding and casting, and Tundra Designs printed and finished the pieces of the suit. The finished full-body costume "is quite comfy to wear and movement is great. I can't bend at the stomach, but I didn't expect that," Dee said in

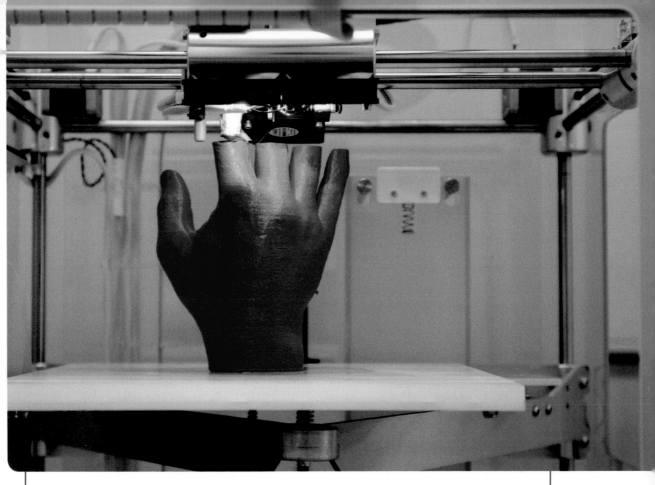

3D printing allows for the creation of extremely lifelike builds of video game and anime costumes.

an interview with 3DPrint.com. Purchasing a 3D printer (which costs anywhere from $300 to $30,000 depending on type and quality) may be out of the question for most cosplayers, but that doesn't mean the tech is out of reach entirely. Even if you don't know how to use 3D modeling programs, websites such as Thingiverse and MyMiniFactory offer open-source models for download. Provided with a model, 3D printing services such as Shapeways and Sculpteo can bring a moderately sized prop to life. Once the model is printed, the job still needs to be sanded and painted to look lifelike.

MEAGAN MARIE'S WARRIOR WONDER WOMAN

To bring her vision of a Greek Goddess Warrior version of Wonder Woman to life, cosplayer Meagan Marie collaborated with artist Tess Fowler to create an original design, patterned extensively on paper, cut and dyed leather patterns, and shaped thermoplastic armor pieces. With help, she learned to use an industrial sewing machine to make a leather corset for the costume. She riveted the pieces of the costume together and built, painted, and distressed convention-safe sword and shield accessories. She made a cape from an oversized circular tablecloth and finally styled a wig to achieve the hairstyle she envisioned before finally debuting the iconic costume at the Salón del Ocio y la Fantasía (SOFA) convention in Bogota, Columbia, in 2012. "I've always adored Diana's [Wonder Woman's] Amazon roots, and wanted to pay tribute to that aspect of her legacy," Marie wrote in a post on her blog. As the ferocious photos of the finished costume show, the diligence and hard work Marie poured into the costume's creation certainly succeeded in emphasizing the character's might.

DO IT ALL FOR LOVE

Craft is the heart and soul of cosplay, the process by which cosplayers show their love and appreciation for the characters they imitate. As a hobby, cosplay welcomes people of all skill levels. But on a professional level, only those who are truly passionate about the laborious process of costume making dedicate their

"Commander" Holly Conrad is known for creating elaborate and authentic costumes.

time and skill to working in cosplay part- or full-time. Some cosplayers, like Meagan Marie, don't want to earn money from their cosplay work. "I fear that if I start to monetize my work it will detract from the real reason I do what I do. I cosplay because I love it, it challenges me, and it lets me express my fandom," Marie wrote. Others, like Linda Le, use the money they earn from cosplay to fund future costumes and cosplay outings. In either case, everyone who works to create professional-grade cosplay costumes is motivated by a deep love of the art form. "Do it because you love it, not because of any other reason," advised pro monster-maker and cosplayer Holly Conrad. "And use the right glue for the right situation."

commission An order for the production of a specific costume or accessory from a professional costumer.

convention (con) A fan gathering at which cosplayers gather to interact with each other and the writers, artists, and actors who create media they enjoy.

#cospositive A social media hashtag that demonstrates support and acceptance for cosplayers of all body types.

harassment Aggressive pressure or intimidation through verbal or written insults and threats, inappropriate touching or picture taking, or lewd propositions.

pauldron A piece of armor at the shoulder and top of the arm that sometimes overlaps the back and chest.

sponsored appearance When a company pays a cosplayer to make an appearance at a convention or event in association with the company's brand.

thermoplastic A plastic material that becomes pliable or moldable above a specific temperature and solidifies upon cooling.

3D printing The process of making three-dimensional solid objects from a digital file by adding successive layers of material until the entire object is created.

urethane Short for polyurethane, a synthetic product that is often used as a part of a varnish.

vacuform A process that molds a plastic sheet into a certain shape.

zine A small, usually self-published fan magazine, commonly used to share thoughts between sci-fi and fantasy fans in the years before Internet access became popular.

Anime North
650 Dixon Road
Toronto, ON M9W 1J1
Canada
(416) 245-5000
Website: http://www.animenorth.com/live
Anime North is Canada's premier fan-run anime convention.

Comic-Con International: San Diego
8340 Allison Avenue
La Mesa, CA 91942
(619) 414-1020
Website: http://www.comic-con.org
Comic-Con International: San Diego is a not-for-profit edu-
    cational organization that strives to create "awareness of,
    and appreciation for, comics and related popular artforms,"
    primarily through conventions and events.

Dragon*Con
P.O. Box 16459
Atlanta, GA 30321-0459
(404) 669-0773
Website: http://www.dragoncon.org
Dragon*Con is an annual pop culture fan convention held in
    Atlanta, Georgia.

Fan Expo Canada
10 Alcorn Avenue, Suite 100
Toronto, ON M4V 3A9

Canada
Website: http://fanexpocanada.com
Fan Expo Canada is the third-largest pop culture event in
    North America.

FanimeCon
150 W San Carlos Street
San Jose, CA 95113
(408) 295-9600
Website: http://www.fanime.com
"By fans, for fans," FanimeCon is Northern California's largest
    anime convention.

New York City Comic Con
655 West 34th Street
New York, NY 10001
(888) 605-6059
Website: http://www.newyorkcomiccon.com
New York City Comic Con, held annually at the Javits Center, is
    the largest pop culture fan convention in the United States.

WEBSITES

Because of the changing nature of Internet links, Rosen Pub-
    lishing has developed an online list of websites related
    to the subject of this book. This site is updated regularly.
    Please use this link to access the list:

http://www.rosenlinks.com/RPFP/Cos

Alinger, Brandon. *Star Wars Costumes*. San Francisco, CA: Chronicle Books, 2014.

Ashcraft, Brian, and Luke Plunkett. *Cosplay World*. Munich, Germany: Prestel, 2014.

Block, Paula, and Terry Erdmann. *Star Trek: Costumes: Five Decades of Fashion from the Final Frontier*. San Rafael, CA: Insight Editions, 2015.

Han, Yaya, and Allison DeBlasio. *1,000 Incredible Costume and Cosplay Ideas: A Showcase of Creative Characters from Anime, Manga, Video Games, Movies, Comics, and More*. Minneapolis, MN: Rockport Publishers, 2013.

Lunning, Frenchy, and Joanne Eicher. *Cosplay: Fashion & Fandom (Dress, Body, Culture)*. New York, NY: Bloomsbury Academic, 2016.

Orsini, Lauren. *Cosplay*. London, England: Carlton Books Ltd., 2015.

Sekeris, Constantine, Carlo Arellano, and Phillip Boutte. *Costume Design & Illustration: For Film, Video Games and Animation*. Culver City, CA: Design Studio Press, 2014.

Takahara, Miyuu, and Kenji Weston. *Cosplay: The Beginner's Masterclass (Beginner's Masterclasses Book 3)*. Charleston, SC: Triangle Square Circle, 2015.

Takasou, Yuki. *Cosplay Basics: A Beginners Guide to the Art of Costume Play*. Long Island City, NY: One Peace Books, 2015.

Williamson, Kyle J. *Elements of Cosplay: The Costume and Beyond*. Charleston, SC: CreateSpace Publishing Platform, 2015.

Wolfe, Brian, and Nick Wolfe. *Extreme Costume Makeup: 25 Creepy & Cool Step-by-Step Demos*. Cincinnati, OH: Impact, 2013.

Ackerman, Forrest J. "I Remember Morojo." 1965. Retrieved March 10, 2015 (http://ww.efanzines.com/Morojo/Morojo-AnAppreciation-1965.pdf).

Bertram, Colin. "Comic-Con: The Power and Politics of Cosplay." NBC Bay Area. July 25, 2014. Retrieved March 10, 2015 (http://www.nbcbayarea.com/entertainment/entertainment-news/Comic-Con-Cosplay-the-Power-and-Politics--268627532.html).

Cardenas, Richard. "Meet the Cast: SyFy's Heroes of Cosplay—Jessica Merizan & Holly Conrad." Pop Cults. August 12, 2013. Retrieved May 25, 2015 (http://www.popcults.com/meet-the-cast-syfys-heroes-of-cosplay-jessica-merizan-holly-conrad/).

Dark-Star, Abby. "The Cosplay Money Fallacy." KeAbtium. November 28, 2014. Retrieved May 25, 2015 (http://www.keabtium.com/the-cosplay-money-fallacy/).

Duncan, Randy, and Matthew J. Smith, eds. *Icons of the American Comic Book, Volume 1*. Santa Barbara, CA: ABC-CLIO, 2013.

Elyse, Lindsay. I Am Lindsay Elyse, Professional Cosplayer. AMA!. Reddit. October 25, 2014. Retrieved March 10, 2015 (https://www.reddit.com/r/IAmA/comments/2kb5ir/i_am_lindsay_elyse_professional_cosplayer_ama/).

Granshaw, Lisa. "Investigating the 'Psychology of Cosplay.'" The Daily Dot. November 11, 2013. Retrieved April 5, 2015 (http://www.dailydot.com/fandom/psychology-cosplay-survey-results/).

Jeffries, Adrianne. "Being Spider Girl: A Day at Comic-Con with a Master of Make-believe." The Verge. July 22, 2013. Retrieved March 10, 2015 (http://www.theverge.com/2013/7/22/4544506/the-life-of-a-professional-cosplayer-at-comic-con-linda-le).

Levine, Ken. "We Love Our BioShock Cosplayers So Much We Hired One!" Irrational Games. December 2, 2012. Retrieved March 10, 2015 (http://irrationalgames.com/insider/we-love-our-bioshock-cosplayers-so-much-we-hired-one/).

Lien, Tracey. "No Girls Allowed." Polygon. December 2, 2013. Retrieved March 10, 2015 (http://www.polygon.com/features/2013/12/2/5143856/no-girls-allowed).

Lynn, Samara. "How to 3D Print Your Cosplay Costume. PC News." October 13, 2014. Retrieved April 20, 2015 (http://www.pcmag.com/article2/0,2817,2470311,00.asp).

Maggs, Sam. "Another Comic Book Artist Can't Stand Change, Competition; Writes Whiny Post About Cosplayers." The Mary Sue. December 5, 2014. Retrieved May 25, 2015 (http://www.themarysue.com/comic-book-artist-slams-cosplay-again/).

Marie, Meagan. "Cosplay Feature: Warrior Wonder Woman." Meagan-Marie. com. October 23, 2013. Retrieved March 10, 2015 (http://www. meagan-marie.com/warriorwonderwoman/).

O'Brien, Christopher M. The Forrest J Ackerman Oeuvre. Jefferson, NC: McFarland & Company Inc., 2012.

Ohanesian, Liz. "Cosplay Is Not Consent: Anime Conventions Attack the Problem of Harassment." LA Weekly, January 10, 2013. Retrieved March 10, 2015 (http://www.laweekly.com/arts/cosplay-is-not-consent-anime-conventions-attack-the-problem-of-harassment-4184027).

Raymond, Adam K. "75 Years of Capes and Face Paint: A History of Cosplay." Yahoo! Movies. 2014. Retrieved March 10, 2015 (https://www.yahoo.com/movies/75-years-of-capes-and-face-paint-a-history-of-cosplay-92666923267.html).

Resnick, Mike. ...Always a Fan: True Stories from a Life in Science Fiction. Rockville, MD: Wildside Press, 2009.

Silverstein, Jonathan. "Sexy 'Booth Babes' Under Siege." ABC News. February 2, 2006. Retrieved April 20, 2015 (http://abcnews.go.com/Technology/story?id=1558683).

Steigerwald, Barbara. "Interview with the One and Only D-Piddy." When Nerds Attack. March 7, 2013. Retrieved May 25, 2015 (http://whennerdsattack. com/2013/03/07/interview-with-the-one-and-only-d-piddy/).

White, Kaila. "Two Metro Phoenix Women Make Cosplay a Career." The Arizona Republic, azcentral.com. June 4, 2014. Retrieved April 20, 2015 (http://www.azcentral.com/story/entertainment/events/2014/05/31/two-metro-phoenix-women-make-cosplay-career/9738879/).

Winge, Theresa. Costuming the Imagination: Origins of Anime and Manga Cosplay. Minneapolois, MN: University of Minnesota Press, 2006.

Yunie. "Interview with Jezeroth." Cosplay Blog...with a Brain. October 8, 2011. Retrieved May 25, 2015 (https://cosplaybrain.wordpress.com/2011/10/08/interview-with-jezeroth/).

About the Author

Jennifer Culp is an author of nonfiction books for children and young adults and a video game enthusiast. Her writing about video games has appeared in national and international publications.

Photo Credits

Cover starmaro/Shutterstock.com; pp. 4, 18, 27 Albert L. Ortega/Getty Images; p. 7 Jeff Kravitz/FilmMagic, Inc/Getty Images; p. 10 Toru Yamanaka/AFP/Getty Images; p. 11 Matteo Valle/Getty Images; p. 14 Neilson Barnard/Getty Images; p. 17 Daniel Zuchnik/Getty Images; p. 22 Ethan Miller/Getty Images; p. 24 Daniel Sims/Getty Images; p. 30 Matthew Lloyd/Getty Images; p. 33 MilanMarkowvic78/Shutterstock.com; p. 35 Shirlaine Forrest/Getty Images; p. 37 © iStockphoto.com/dreamnikon; p. 39 Sean Gallup/Getty Images
Designer: Brian Garvey; Editor/Photo Researcher: Heather Moore Niver